CW00517200

Healthiest ways to Cook for Diabetics

Delicious an Easy Diabetic Recipes for Everyone

Evelin Turk

All rights reserved. Copyright 2021.

Table of Contents

Raspberry Granita

Servings: 6

Ingredients:

1 cup water 1/3 cup sugar

1 (12-ounce) package frozen unsweetened raspberries, thawed

1 tablespoon lemon juice

Directions:

1. Cook the water and sugar in a small saucepan over medium heat, until the sugar dissolves. Cool to room temperature.

2. Place the raspberries and lemon juice in a food processor and process until smooth. Press the mixture through a fine wire mesh strainer, discarding the solids. Combine the sugar syrup and the raspberry mixture in a shallow glass baking dish and stir to mix well.

3. Freeze, stirring every 15 minutes, until the granita is almost firm, about 2 hours. Freeze without stirring until firm, 2 hours or overnight.

4. When ready to serve, let stand at room temperature 10 minutes. Scrape the granita with a fork to break it into crystals. Serve at once. The granita can be frozen for 1 week.

Nutrition Info:

16 g carb, 63 cal, 0 g fat, 0 g sat fat, 0 mg chol, 1 g fib, 0 g pro, 7 mg sod • Carb Choices: 1; Exchanges: 1 carb

Creamy Chicken Fettuccini

Servings: 4

Ingredients:

4 ounces whole wheat fettuccini

2 (4-ounce) skinless boneless chicken breasts

1/2 teaspoon kosher salt, divided

1/4 teaspoon freshly ground pepper, divided

4 teaspoons extra virgin olive oil, divided

1 medium red bell pepper, thinly sliced

1 medium yellow bell pepper, thinly sliced

1 small zucchini, halved lengthwise and sliced

1 small red onion, halved lengthwise and thinly sliced

2 garlic cloves, minced

21/2 ounces reduced-fat cream cheese (about 1/3 cup), at room temperature, cut into small pieces

3 tablespoons chopped fresh Italian parsley

2 teaspoons grated lemon zest

Directions:

1. Cook the pasta according to the package directions. Drain in a colander, reserving 1/2 cup of the cooking water.

2. Meanwhile, sprinkle the chicken with 1/4 teaspoon of the salt and 1/8 teaspoon of the ground pepper. Heat a large nonstick skillet over medium heat. Add 2 teaspoons of the oil and tilt the pan to coat the bottom evenly. Add the chicken and cook, turning once, until the juices run clear, about 4 minutes on each side. Transfer to a plate.

3. Increase the heat to medium-high. Add the remaining 2 teaspoons oil to the skillet and tilt the pan to coat the bottom evenly. Add the bell peppers, zucchini, and onion and cook, stirring often, until crisp-tender, about 3 minutes. Add the garlic and cook, stirring constantly, until fragrant, 30 seconds.

4. Thinly slice the chicken breasts and add to the skillet. Remove from the heat and add the pasta and cream cheese and toss to combine, adding the reserved pasta cooking water 1 tablespoon at a time, as need to make a smooth sauce. Stir in the remaining 1/4 teaspoon salt, remaining 1/8 teaspoon ground pepper, the parsley, and lemon zest. Divide evenly among 4 serving plates and serve at once.

Nutrition Info:

28 g carb, 274 cal, 10 g fat, 4 g sat fat, 44 mg chol, 6 g fib, 19 g pro, 253 mg sod • Carb Choices: 2; Exchanges: 11/2 starch, 1 veg, 2 lean protein, 1 fat

Tuna with Cilantro-citrus Sauce

Servings: 4

Ingredients:

SAUCE

1 cup tightly packed fresh cilantro leaves

1/4 cup orange juice

2 tablespoons extra virgin olive oil

1 tablespoon lime juice

1/4 teaspoon ground cumin

1/8 teaspoon kosher salt

Pinch of ground cayenne

FISH

4 (5-ounce) tuna steaks

1/2 teaspoon ground cumin

1/4 teaspoon kosher salt

Pinch of ground cayenne

2 teaspoons extra virgin olive oil

Directions:

1. To make the sauce, combine all the ingredients in a food processor and process until smooth.

2. To make the fish, sprinkle the tuna with the cumin, salt, and cayenne. Heat a large skillet over medium-high heat. Add the oil and tilt the pan to coat the bottom evenly. Add the tuna and cook, turning once, 2 minutes on each side for medium rare, or to the desired degree of doneness. Place the tuna on 4 plates, drizzle evenly with the sauce, and serve at once.

Nutrition Info:

2 g carb, 242 cal, 10 g fat, 1 g sat fat, 62 mg chol, 0 g fib, 32 g pro, 158 mg sod •
Carb Choices: 0; Exchanges: 4 lean protein, 1 fat

Spinach Stracciatella

Servings: 4

Ingredients:

4 cups Chicken Stock or low-sodium chicken broth

1 small garlic clove, crushed through a press

1/2 teaspoon kosher salt

1 large egg, lightly beaten

2 cups thinly sliced fresh spinach

1 ounce freshly grated Parmigiano-Reggiano (about 1/4 cup)

2 teaspoons lemon juice

Pinch of freshly ground pepper

Directions:

1. Combine the stock, garlic, and salt in a medium pot and bring to a boil over high heat.

2. Slowly drizzle the egg into the stock mixture, stirring constantly. Turn off the heat and stir in the spinach, Parmigiano-Reggiano, lemon juice, and pepper. Ladle the soup into 4 bowls and serve at once. The soup is best when eaten immediately.

Nutrition Info:

2 g carb, 70 cal, 3 g fat, 2 g sat fat, 62 mg chol, 0 g fib, 8 g pro, 386 mg sod • Carb Choices: 0; Exchanges: 1/2 lean protein

Flan

Servings: 12

Ingredients:

1 teaspoon canola oil

1/2 cup granulated sugar

2 tablespoons water

2 (12-ounce) cans fat-free evaporated milk

1/2 cup packed light brown sugar

3 large eggs

2 large egg whites

1 teaspoon vanilla extract

Directions:

1. Preheat the oven to 350°F. Brush the inside rim of a 9-inch round cake pan with the oil, leaving the bottom of the pan uncoated.

2. Stir together the granulated sugar and water in a medium saucepan. Cook over medium heat, stirring constantly, until the sugar dissolves, about 3 minutes. Continue cooking, without stirring, until the mixture turns golden, about 6 minutes longer. Carefully pour the sugar mixture into the prepared pan, tilting the pan to coat the bottom (the pan will be hot after pouring in the caramel).

3. Whisk together the evaporated milk, brown sugar, eggs, egg whites, and vanilla in a large bowl. Pour into the cake pan. Place the cake pan inside a large roasting pan and add hot water to the pan halfway up the side of the cake pan.

4. Bake until a knife inserted in the edge of the flan comes out clean and flan is still soft in the center, 45 to 50 minutes. Carefully remove the flan from the water bath and cool on a wire rack for 1 hour. Refrigerate the flan, covered, overnight.

5. To serve, run a small spatula around the edge of the flan and invert onto a rimmed serving plate to avoid spilling the syrup.

Nutrition Info:

25 g carb, 137 cal, 2 g fat, 0 g sat fat, 53 mg chol, 0 g fib, 6 g pro, 101 mg sod •
Carb Choices: 1 1/2; Exchanges: 1 1/2 carb

Feta Cheese Spread

Servings: 1

Ingredients:

2 ounces crumbled feta cheese, at room temperature (about 1/2 cup)

1/2 cup reduced-fat cream cheese, cut into small pieces, at room temperature

2 tablespoons minced scallion

2 tablespoons chopped fresh Italian parsley

2 teaspoons grated lemon zest

1 tablespoon lemon juice

Directions:

1. Combine all the ingredients in a food processor and process until the mixture is smooth. The spread can be refrigerated, covered, for up to 3 days.

Nutrition Info:

2 g carb, 61 cal, 5 g fat, 3 g sat fat, 17 mg chol, 0 g fib, 3 g pro, 150 mg sod • Carb Choices: 0; Exchanges: 1 fat

Wheat Berries with Fennel And Apple

Servings: 6

Ingredients:

2 teaspoons extra virgin olive oil

1/2 cup chopped fennel bulb

1 small Granny Smith apple, peeled, cored, and chopped

2 cups cooked wheat berries

2 tablespoons water

1 tablespoon chopped fresh Italian parsley

1 teaspoon lemon juice

1/2 teaspoon kosher salt

Pinch of freshly ground pepper

Directions:

1. Heat a medium nonstick skillet over medium heat. Add the oil and tilt the pan to coat the bottom evenly. Add the fennel and cook, stirring often, until softened, 5 minutes. Add the apple and cook, stirring often, until the apple just begins to soften, 3 minutes.

2. Add the wheat berries and water. Cook, stirring often until the wheat berries are heated through, about 2 minutes. Remove from the heat and stir in the parsley, lemon juice, salt, and pepper. Spoon the wheat berries into a serving dish and serve at once.

Nutrition Info:

21 g carb, 118 cal, 2 g fat, 0 g sat fat, 0 mg chol, 3 g fib, 4 g pro, 98 mg sod • Carb Choices: 1 1⁄2; Exchanges: 1 1⁄2 starch

Chicken, Chorizo, And Rice Casserole

Servings: 4

Ingredients:

3 teaspoons canola oil, divided

1/2 cup long-grain brown rice

12 ounces boneless skinless chicken thighs, cut into 1-inch pieces

1/4 teaspoon kosher salt

1/2 teaspoon paprika

1/4 teaspoon freshly ground pepper

2 ounces cured chorizo, casings removed, chopped

1 small onion, chopped

1 small red bell pepper, chopped

1 stalk celery, chopped

2 garlic cloves, minced

3/4 cup Chicken Stock or low-sodium chicken broth

1 (141/2-ounce) can no-salt-added diced tomatoes

Directions:

1. Preheat the oven to 375°F. Brush an 11 x 7-inch baking dish with 1 teaspoon of the oil. Spread the rice in the prepared dish.

2. Sprinkle the chicken with the salt, paprika, and ground pepper. Heat a large nonstick skillet over medium-high heat. Add the remaining 2 teaspoons oil and tilt the pan to coat the bottom evenly. Add the chicken and cook, stirring often, until well browned, about 6 minutes. Transfer to the baking dish with the rice.

3. Add the sausage to the skillet and cook, turning often, until well browned, 4 minutes. Transfer to the baking dish with the chicken. Drain off and discard most of the drippings in the skillet, leaving the skillet just lightly coated.

4. Add the onion, bell pepper, and celery to the skillet and cook, stirring often, until softened, 5 minutes. Add the garlic and cook, stirring constantly, until fragrant, 30 seconds. Add the stock and tomatoes and bring to a boil, stirring to scrape up the browned bits from the bottom of the skillet. Carefully pour the vegetable mixture over the chicken and sausage in the baking dish. Cover the dish tightly with foil and bake 1 hour. Let stand, covered, for 15 minutes before serving. Spoon evenly into 4 plates and serve at once.

Nutrition Info:

28 g carb, 348 cal, 16 g fat, 4 g sat fat, 70 mg chol, 4 g fib, 23 g pro, 371 mg sod • Carb Choices: 2; Exchanges: 1½ starch, 1 veg, 3 lean protein, 2 fat

Cucumber-dill Potato Salad

Servings: 4

Ingredients:

1 pound red-skinned or other waxy potatoes, well scrubbed

2 tablespoons mayonnaise

2 tablespoons plain low-fat yogurt

1 tablespoon lemon juice

1 teaspoon kosher salt

1/8 teaspoon freshly ground pepper

1/2 hothouse (English) cucumber, halved lengthwise and thinly sliced

1 thin scallion, thinly sliced

2 tablespoons chopped fresh dill

Directions:

1. Place the potatoes in a large saucepan. Add water to cover and bring to a boil over high heat. Reduce the heat to low and simmer, uncovered, until the potatoes are tender, 15 to 20 minutes. Drain and let stand until cool enough to handle. Cut the potatoes into 1-inch pieces.

2. Meanwhile, whisk together the mayonnaise, yogurt, lemon juice, salt, and pepper in a large bowl. Add the potatoes, cucumber, scallion, and dill and toss to combine. Serve the salad at room temperature or chilled. The salad tastes best on the day it is made, but it can be refrigerated, covered, for up to 1 day.

Nutrition Info:

20 g carb, 142 cal, 6 g fat, 1 g sat fat, 3 mg chol, 2 g fib, 3 g pro, 331 mg sod • Carb Choices: 1; Exchanges: 1 1/2 starch, 1 fat

Roasted Eggplant with Tomato Vinaigrette

Servings: 6

Ingredients:

1 teaspoon plus 3 tablespoons extra virgin olive oil, divided

1 large eggplant (about 13⁄4 pounds), cut into 1⁄2-inch rounds

1⁄2 teaspoon kosher salt, divided

1⁄4 teaspoon freshly ground pepper, divided

1 tablespoon red wine vinegar

1 garlic clove, crushed through a press

1⁄2 teaspoon Dijon mustard

1⁄4 cup peeled diced fresh tomato

2 teaspoons chopped fresh rosemary

Directions:

1. Preheat the oven to 425°F. Brush a large rimmed baking sheet with 1 teaspoon of the oil.

2. Brush the eggplant slices with 1 tablespoon of the remaining oil. Sprinkle with 1/4 teaspoon of the salt and 1/8 teaspoon of the pepper. Arrange in a single layer on the baking sheet. Bake, turning once, until tender and well browned, 35 to 40 minutes.

3. Meanwhile, whisk together the vinegar, garlic, mustard, remaining 1/4 teaspoon salt, and remaining 1/8 teaspoon pepper in a medium bowl. Slowly whisk in the remaining 2 tablespoons oil. Stir in the tomato and rosemary.

4. To serve, arrange the eggplant slices on a serving platter. Spoon the vinaigrette evenly over the eggplant. Serve hot, warm, or at room temperature.

Nutrition Info:

8 g carb, 97 cal, 7 g fat, 1 g sat fat, 0 mg chol, 5 g fib, 1 g pro, 108 mg sod • Carb Choices: 1/2; Exchanges: 1 veg, 11/2 fat

Chocolate Layer Cake with Fluffy White Frosting

Servings: 12

Ingredients:

1 recipe Chocolate Cake

1 recipe Fluffy White Frosting

Directions:

1. Prepare the cake recipe, baking the cake in round cake pans. To do so, line two 8- or 9-inch round cake pans with parchment paper. Brush the sides of the pans with the 2 teaspoons butter. Spoon the batter evenly into the pans. Bake 8-inch cakes for 25 minutes and 9-inch cakes for 23 minutes.

2. Cool the cakes in the pans on a wire rack for 10 minutes. Remove from the pans and cool completely on a wire rack. Spread the frosting between the layers and on the sides and top of the cake.

Nutrition Info:

38 g carb, 222 cal, 8 g fat, 5 g sat fat, 43 mg chol, 2 g fib, 4 g pro, 151 mg sod •
Carb Choices: 21/2; Exchanges: 21/2 carb, 11/2 fat

Cheddar-stuffed Turkey Burgers

Servings: 4

Ingredients:

4 ounces white mushrooms

1 pound ground lean turkey

1/4 cup plain dry breadcrumbs

1 large egg white

1 garlic clove, minced

2 teaspoons chili powder

1/2 teaspoon cumin

1/4 teaspoon kosher salt

1/4 teaspoon freshly ground pepper

1 ounce finely shredded reduced-fat extra-sharp

Cheddar cheese (about 1/4 cup)

2 teaspoons canola oil

4 whole wheat kaiser rolls, split and toasted

4 large leaves leaf lettuce

3/4 cup Fresh Tomato Salsa or purchased tomato salsa

Directions:

1. Place the mushrooms in a food processor and pulse until finely chopped.

2. Combine the mushrooms, turkey, breadcrumbs, egg white, garlic, chili powder, cumin, salt, and pepper in a medium bowl and mix thoroughly with your hands. Shape into 8 patties. Place 1 tablespoon of the Cheddar on top of each of 4 of the patties. Top with the remaining 4 patties and pinch the edges to seal.

3. Heat a large nonstick skillet over medium-high heat. Add the oil and tilt the pan to coat the bottom evenly. Add the burgers and cook, turning once, until no longer pink, 5 minutes on each side. Serve the burgers in the rolls, topped with the lettuce and salsa.

Nutrition Info:

30 g carb, 319 cal, 12 g fat, 3 g sat fat, 54 mg chol, 4 g fib, 25 g pro, 468 mg sod •
Carb Choices: 2; Exchanges: 2 starch, 3 lean protein, 1 fat

Lemon-garlic Pita Chips

Servings: 8

Ingredients:

1 tablespoon extra virgin olive oil

1 garlic clove, crushed through a press

1 teaspoon grated lemon zest

2 (6-inch) whole wheat pita breads

1/8 teaspoon kosher salt

Directions:

1. Preheat the oven to 350°F.

2. Combine the oil and garlic in a small saucepan and set over medium heat just until hot, about 2 minutes. Stir in the lemon zest.

3. Split each pita in half to make 4 rounds. Brush the rough side of the rounds with the oil mixture. Cut each round into 12 wedges. Place the pita wedges in a single layer rough side up on a large baking sheet and sprinkle with the salt.

4. Bake until the pita wedges are crisp and lightly toasted, 10 to 12 minutes. Cool the chips in the pan on a wire rack. The chips can be covered in an airtight container and stored at room temperature for up to 5 days.

Nutrition Info:

9 g carb, 59 cal, 2 g fat, 0 g sat fat, 0 mg chol, 1 g fib, 2 g pro, 103 mg sod • Carb Choices: 1/2; Exchanges: 1/2 starch, 1/2 fat

Grilled Scallops with Ponzu Sauce

Servings: 4

Ingredients:

2 tablespoons lime juice

2 tablespoons lemon juice

2 tablespoons reduced-sodium soy sauce

1 tablespoon mirin

1 tablespoon sugar

1/4 teaspoon Asian fish sauce

1 pound sea scallops

1/2 teaspoon canola oil Thinly sliced scallions

Chopped fresh cilantro

Directions:

1. Preheat the grill to medium-high heat.

2. Whisk together the lime juice, lemon juice, soy sauce, mirin, sugar, and fish sauce in a small bowl.

3. Place the scallops in a medium shallow dish. Add 1 tablespoon of the sauce and toss to coat. Cover and refrigerate 15 minutes.

4. Brush the grill rack with the oil. Remove the scallops from the marinade and discard the marinade. Pat the scallops dry and place on the grill. Grill, turning once, just until the scallops are opaque in the center, 2 to 3 minutes.

5. Divide the scallops among 4 plates and drizzle with the remaining sauce. Sprinkle with the scallions and cilantro and serve at once.

Nutrition Info:

9 g carb, 134 cal, 1 g fat, 0 g sat fat, 37 mg chol, 0 g fib, 20 g pro, 514 mg sod • Carb Choices: 1/2; Exchanges: 1/2 carb, 3 lean protein

Sugar Snap Peas with Ginger And Orange

Servings: 4

Ingredients:

2 teaspoons grated fresh ginger

2 teaspoons unsalted butter

1 teaspoon grated orange zest

1/2 teaspoon kosher salt

1-pound fresh sugar snap peas, trimmed

Directions:

1. Stir together the ginger, butter, orange zest, and salt in a medium serving bowl. Set aside.

2. Bring a large saucepan of water to a boil over high heat. Add the peas and cook until just crisp-tender, 1 minute. Drain in a colander.

3. Add the peas to the ginger mixture and toss gently to coat. Serve at once.

Nutrition Info:

10 g carb, 71 cal, 2 g fat, 1 g sat fat, 5 mg chol, 3 g fib, 3 g pro, 154 mg sod • Carb Choices: 1/2; Exchanges: 2 veg, 1/2 fat

Turkey Mole Chili

Servings: 6

Ingredients:

2 teaspoons extra virgin olive oil

1 pound ground extra-lean turkey

1 large onion, chopped

1 large red bell pepper, chopped

2 garlic cloves, minced

2 tablespoons chili powder

2 tablespoons ground cumin

1/2 teaspoon dried oregano

1 cup brewed coffee

2 cups Chicken Stock or low-sodium chicken broth

1 (15-ounce) can no-salt-added black beans, rinsed and drained

1 (141/2-ounce) can no-salt-added diced tomatoes

2 tablespoons no-salt-added tomato paste

2 tablespoons unsweetened cocoa

1/4 teaspoon kosher salt

2 tablespoons lime juice

1 tablespoon honey Thinly sliced scallions

Chopped fresh cilantro

Directions:

1. Heat a large saucepan over medium-high heat. Add the oil and tilt the pan to coat the bottom evenly. Add the turkey, onion, and bell pepper and cook, stirring often, until the turkey is no longer pink, 8 minutes. Add the garlic, chili powder, cumin, and oregano and cook, stirring constantly, until fragrant, 30 seconds.

2. Add the coffee, stock, beans, tomatoes, tomato paste, cocoa, and salt and bring to a boil. Reduce the heat to low, cover, and simmer 25 to 30 minutes. Remove from the heat and stir in the lime juice and honey. Divide the chili among 6 bowls and sprinkle each serving with scallions and cilantro. The chili can be refrigerated, covered, for up to 4 days or frozen for up to 3 months.

Nutrition Info:

24 g carb, 214 cal, 4 g fat, 1 g sat fat, 24 mg chol, 7 g fib, 22 g pro, 282 mg sod • Carb Choices: 1½; Exchanges: 1 starch, 1 veg, 3 lean protein

Beer-braised Chicken Sausages with Fennel And Peppers

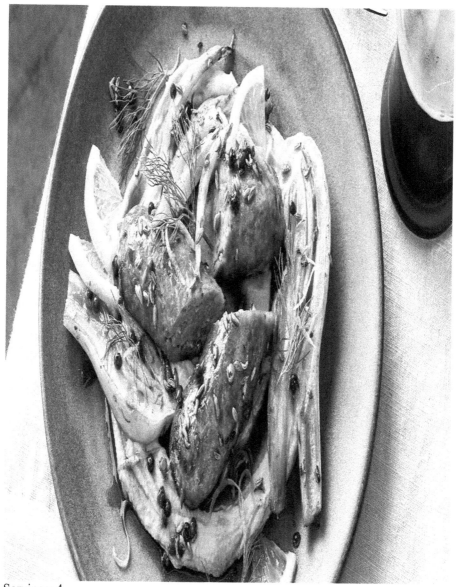

Servings: 4

Ingredients:

1 medium bulb fennel

4 teaspoons extra virgin olive oil, divided

4 links chicken sausage (about 1 pound), halved lengthwise

1 yellow bell pepper, cut into strips

1 medium onion, halved lengthwise and thinly sliced

2 garlic cloves, minced

1 cup lager beer

1 tablespoon light brown sugar

1/4 cup chopped fresh Italian parsley

Directions:

1. Trim the tough outer stalks from the fennel. Cut the fennel bulb in half vertically and cut away and discard the core. Cut each half lengthwise into 1/4-inch slices.

2. Heat a large nonstick skillet over medium-high heat. Add 2 teaspoons of the oil and tilt the pan to coat the bottom evenly. Add the sausages and cook until well browned on both sides, 4 to 6 minutes. Transfer to a plate.

3. Add the remaining 2 teaspoons oil and tilt the pan to coat the bottom evenly. Add the fennel, bell pepper, and onion and cook, stirring often, until softened, 5 minutes. Add the garlic and cook, stirring constantly, until fragrant, 30 seconds. Place the sausages on top of the vegetables. Pour the beer over the sausages and bring to a boil.

4. Reduce the heat to low, cover, and simmer, stirring occasionally, until the vegetables are tender, about 10 minutes. Uncover and stir in the sugar. Increase the heat to medium-high and cook, stirring often, until most of the liquid is evaporated, about 3 minutes. Transfer the sausages to 4 plates. Stir the parsley into the vegetable mixture and serve with the sausages.

Nutrition Info:

19 g carb, 274 cal, 14 g fat, 3 g sat fat, 75 mg chol, 4 g fib, 16 g pro, 708 mg sod • Carb Choices: 1; Exchanges: 1/2 carb, 2 veg, 2 medium-fat protein, 1 fat

Celery Root Salad with Mustard Dressing

Servings: 4

Ingredients:

1/4 cup plain low-fat Greek yogurt or strained yogurt

1 1/2 tablespoons lemon juice

2 teaspoons whole grain mustard

2 teaspoons extra virgin olive oil

1/4 teaspoon kosher salt

Pinch of freshly ground pepper

1 large celery root, cut into long, thin strips (about 4 cups)

1/4 cup chopped fresh Italian parsley

Directions:

1. Whisk together the yogurt, lemon juice, mustard, oil, salt, and pepper in a large bowl.

2. Add the celery root and parsley and toss to coat. Refrigerate the salad, covered, until chilled, 2 hours or up to 1 day.

Nutrition Info:

13 g carb, 88 cal, 3 g fat, 1 g sat fat, 1 mg chol, 2 g fib, 3 g pro, 250 mg sod • Carb Choices: 1; Exchanges: 2 veg, 1/2 fat

Grilled Caribbean Chicken

Servings: 4

Ingredients:

1/4 cup chopped fresh cilantro

1 jalapeño, including some of the seeds, minced

3 garlic cloves, minced

1 scallion, thinly sliced

2 tablespoons lime juice

2 tablespoons light rum

2 1/2 teaspoons canola oil, divided

1/2 teaspoon ground allspice

4 (4-ounce) boneless skinless chicken breasts

1/2 teaspoon kosher salt

Directions:

1. Combine the cilantro, jalapeño, garlic, scallion, lime juice, rum, 2 teaspoons of the oil, and the allspice in a large resealable plastic bag. Add the chicken, turn to coat, and refrigerate 2 to 4 hours.

2. Preheat the grill to medium-high heat.

3. Remove the chicken from the marinade and discard the marinade. Pat the chicken dry with paper towels and sprinkle with the salt.

4. Brush the grill rack with the remaining 1/2 teaspoon oil. Place the chicken on the grill and grill, turning often, until the juices of the chicken run clear, 8 to 10 minutes. Divide the chicken among 4 plates and serve at once.

Nutrition Info:

1 g carb, 148 cal, 4 g fat, 1 g sat fat, 63 mg chol, 0 g fib, 23 g pro, 195 mg sod • Carb Choices: 0; Exchanges: 3 lean protein

Onion-rye Rolls

Servings: 16

Ingredients:

3 teaspoons extra virgin olive oil, divided

1 cup finely chopped onion

1 cup lukewarm water

1 package active dry yeast

2 cups rye flour

1 to 11/4 cups unbleached all-purpose flour, divided

1 tablespoon sugar

1 teaspoon salt

Directions:

1. Heat a medium nonstick skillet over medium heat. Add 2 teaspoons of the oil and tilt the pan to coat the bottom evenly. Add the onion, cover, and cook, stirring occasionally, until the onion is tender and lightly browned, about 10 minutes. Transfer the onion to a bowl and let stand to cool to room temperature.
2. Combine the water and yeast in a large bowl and stir until the yeast dissolves. Let stand 5 minutes. Add the cooled onion, the rye flour, 1 cup of the all-purpose flour, the sugar, and salt and stir until a soft dough forms.
3. Turn the dough out onto a lightly floured surface. Knead until smooth and elastic, about 8 minutes. Add enough of the remaining 1/4 cup all-purpose flour, 1 tablespoon at a time, to prevent the dough from sticking to your hands. (Alternatively, knead the dough for 5 minutes at low speed with an electric mixer using a dough hook, adding enough of the remaining 1/4 cup all-purpose flour, 1 tablespoon at a time, to make a smooth dough.)
4. Brush a large bowl with the remaining 1 teaspoon oil. Place the dough in the bowl and turn to coat the top. Cover and let rise in a warm place (85°F), free from drafts, until doubled in size, about 1 hour.
5. Line a large baking sheet with parchment paper. Divide the dough into 16 pieces and shape each piece into a ball. Place the balls onto the prepared baking sheet. Cover loosely with lightly oiled plastic wrap and let rise in a warm place (85°F), free from drafts, until doubled in size, about 45 minutes.
6. Preheat the oven to 400°F. Remove the plastic wrap and bake the rolls until lightly browned, 15 to 18 minutes. Transfer to wire racks to cool. Serve warm or at room temperature. The rolls can be stored inside a paper bag at room temperature for up to 2 days or frozen for up to 3 months.

Nutrition Info:

17 g carb, 84 cal, 1 g fat, 0 g sat fat, 0 mg chol, 2 g fib, 2 g pro, 146 mg sod • Carb Choices: 1; Exchanges: 1 starch

Lemon-mint Meatball Soup

Servings: 8

Ingredients:

4 teaspoons extra virgin olive oil, divided

1 pound 95% lean ground beef

1 large egg

1/3 cup plain dry breadcrumbs

1/4 cup chopped fresh mint

1/4 cup chopped fresh Italian parsley

2 garlic cloves, minced

1 tablespoon freshly grated lemon zest

1/4 teaspoon kosher salt

1/2 teaspoon freshly ground pepper

2 carrots, peeled and chopped

1 medium onion, chopped

1 stalk celery, chopped

5 cups Chicken Stock or low-sodium chicken broth

1 (14 1/2-ounce) can no-salt-added diced tomatoes

1/2 cup whole wheat orzo

8 ounces Swiss chard, tough stems removed and leaves chopped

4 tablespoons freshly grated Parmesan

Directions:

1. Preheat the oven to 400°F. Brush a large rimmed baking sheet with 2 teaspoons of the oil.
2. Combine the beef, egg, breadcrumbs, mint, parsley, garlic, lemon zest, salt, and pepper in a large bowl and mix well with your hands. Shape into 1/2- inch meatballs. Place on the prepared pan and bake until browned, 20 to 25 minutes.
3. Meanwhile, heat a large pot over medium heat. Add the oil and tilt the pan to coat the bottom. Add the carrots, onion, and celery and cook until softened, 5 minutes. Add the stock and tomatoes and bring to a boil. Stir in the orzo and return to a boil.
4. Cover, reduce the heat to low, and simmer, stirring occasionally, until the orzo is almost tender, about 10 minutes. Carefully add the meatballs and the chard and cook until the chard is tender, about 5 minutes longer. Ladle into 8 bowls, sprinkle evenly with the Parmesan, and serve at once. The soup can be refrigerated, covered, for up to 4 days.

Nutrition Info:

16 g carb, 202 cal, 7 g fat, 2 g sat fat, 65 mg chol, 3 g fib, 18 g pro, 311 mg sod • Carb Choices: 1; Exchanges: 1 starch, 1 1/2 lean protein, 1/2 fat

Broiled Fish Fillets with Lemon Butter

Servings: 4

Ingredients:

1/2 teaspoon canola oil

4 (5-ounce) thin white-fleshed fish fillets

1/4 teaspoon plus pinch of kosher salt, divided

1/8 teaspoon freshly ground pepper

2 tablespoons unsalted butter, softened

1 teaspoon grated lemon zest

1/2 teaspoon lemon juice Lemon wedges

Directions:

1. Preheat the broiler. Brush a medium rimmed baking sheet with the oil.

2. Sprinkle the fish with 1/4 teaspoon of the salt and the pepper and arrange in a single layer on the prepared baking sheet. Broil, without turning, until the fish flakes easily with a fork, about 8 minutes.

3. Meanwhile, stir together the butter, lemon zest, lemon juice, and remaining pinch of salt in a small bowl. Transfer the fish to 4 plates using a wide spatula, top with the butter mixture, and serve at once with the lemon wedges.

Nutrition Info:

0 g carb, 170 cal, 8 g fat, 4 g sat fat, 82 mg chol, 0 g fib, 24 g pro, 191 mg sod • Carb Choices: 0; Exchanges: 3 lean protein, 1 fat

Slow-cooker Beef Brisket with Onion Gravy

Servings: 12

Ingredients:

1 (3-pound) flat half beef brisket, trimmed of all visible fat

1 teaspoon kosher salt, divided

1/2 teaspoon freshly ground pepper, divided

2 teaspoons extra virgin olive oil

2 medium onions (about 1 pound), halved lengthwise and thinly sliced

1 cup Beef Stock or low-sodium beef broth

2 garlic cloves, minced

2 tablespoons cold water

1 1/2 tablespoons unbleached all-purpose flour

Directions:

1. Sprinkle the brisket with 3/4 teaspoon of the salt and 1/4 teaspoon of the pepper. Heat a large skillet over medium-high heat. Add the oil and tilt the pan to coat the bottom evenly. Add the brisket and cook, turning to brown on both sides, 6 to 8 minutes.

2. Place the onions, stock, garlic, the remaining 1/4 teaspoon salt, and remaining 1/4 teaspoon pepper in a 6-quart oval slow cooker. Place the brisket on top of the onion mixture. Cover and cook on low until the brisket is very tender, 8 hours.

3. Transfer the brisket to a cutting board and cover to keep warm. Whisk together the water and flour in a small bowl. Stir the flour mixture into the stock mixture. Cover and cook on high until the gravy is slightly thickened, about 10 minutes. Slice the roast across the grain into thick slices and divide evenly among 12 plates. Spoon the gravy evenly over the roast and serve at once.

Nutrition Info:

4 g carb, 169 cal, 6 g fat, 2 g sat fat, 49 mg chol, 1 g fib, 24 g pro, 169 mg sod •
Carb Choices: 0; Exchanges: 3 lean protein

Filets Mignons with Cabernet-butter Sauce

Servings: 4

Ingredients:

4 (4-ounce) filets mignons, trimmed of all visible fat

1/2 teaspoon kosher salt

1/8 teaspoon freshly ground pepper

1/2 cup Beef Stock or low-sodium beef broth

1/2 cup Cabernet Sauvignon

1 tablespoon chilled unsalted butter

1/2 teaspoon chopped fresh thyme or 1/8 teaspoon dried thyme

Directions:

1. Sprinkle the steaks with the salt and pepper. Heat a large heavy-bottomed skillet over medium-high heat. Add the steaks to the dry skillet and cook, turning once, 2 minutes on each side for medium-rare, or to the desired degree of doneness. Transfer to a plate and cover loosely with foil to keep warm.

2. Add the stock and wine to the skillet, bring to a boil, and cook until reduced to 3 tablespoons, about 5 minutes. Remove from the heat and whisk in the butter and thyme. Divide the steaks among 4 plates, drizzle evenly with the sauce, and serve at once.

Nutrition Info:

1 g carb, 194 cal, 8 g fat, 4 g sat fat, 60 mg chol, 0 g fib, 23 g pro, 243 mg sod •
Carb Choices: 0; Exchanges: 3 lean protein, 1/2 fat

Bbq Chicken Pizza

Servings: 4

Ingredients:

2 tablespoons light brown sugar

1 teaspoon white wine vinegar

1⁄2 teaspoon minced chipotle in adobo sauce

1 recipe Roasted Red Pepper Pizza Sauce

11⁄2 cups shredded cooked chicken breast

1 prepared Whole Wheat Pizza Crust or 1 (12-inch) purchased prebaked whole wheat thin pizza crust

1⁄4 cup thinly sliced scallions

3 ounces shredded reduced-fat extra-sharp

Cheddar cheese (about 3⁄4 cup)

Directions:

1. Position an oven rack on the lowest rung of the oven. Preheat the oven to 450°F.

2. Add the sugar, vinegar, and chipotle to the pizza sauce and pulse to combine. Transfer 1/4 cup of the sauce to a medium bowl. Add the chicken and toss to coat. Set aside.

3. Place the crust on the bottom rack of the oven and bake 5 minutes.

4. Remove the crust from the oven and spread the remaining sauce evenly over the crust, leaving a 1/2-inch border. Arrange the chicken mixture evenly over the sauce. Sprinkle with the scallions, then with the Cheddar. Bake on the bottom rack until the crust is browned and the cheese melts, about 8 minutes. Cut into 8 wedges and serve at once.

Nutrition Info:

39 g carb, 365 cal, 11 g fat, 4 g sat fat, 60 mg chol, 5 g fib, 28 g pro, 482 mg sod • Carb Choices: 21/2; Exchanges: 2 starch, 1/2 carb, 1 medium-fat protein, 2 lean protein, 1 fat

Goat Cheese And Marinated Red Pepper Bruschetta

Servings: 8

Ingredients:

1 tablespoon balsamic vinegar

1 tablespoon extra virgin olive oil

1 garlic clove, crushed through a press

1/4 teaspoon kosher salt

1/8 teaspoon freshly ground pepper

1 cup red Roasted Bell Peppers or roasted red peppers from a jar, thinly sliced

1 tablespoon capers, rinsed and drained

2 tablespoons chopped fresh basil or Italian parsley

2 ounces goat cheese (about ½ cup), at room temperature

16 (1/4-inch) slices 100% whole wheat baguette, toasted

Directions:

1. Whisk together the vinegar, oil, garlic, salt, and ground pepper in a medium bowl. Add the roasted peppers and capers and stir to combine. Cover and refrigerate at least 8 hours and up to 4 days. Stir in the basil just before serving.

2. To assemble, spread 1/2 tablespoon of the goat cheese on each of the baguette slices. Top the cheese with about 1 tablespoon of the bell pepper mixture. Serve at once.

Nutrition Info:

8 g carb, 84 cal, 4 g fat, 2 g sat fat, 6 mg chol, 2 g fib, 4 g pro, 164 mg sod • Carb Choices: 1/2; Exchanges: 1/2 starch, 1 fat

Black Bean Burritos with Creamy Avocado Sauce

Servings: 4

Ingredients:

2 teaspoons canola oil

1 red bell pepper, thinly sliced

1 medium red onion, thinly sliced

1 jalapeño, seeded and minced

2 garlic cloves, minced

2 teaspoons chili powder

1 teaspoon ground cumin

1 (15-ounce) can no-salt-added black beans, rinsed and drained

1/2 cup Vegetable Stock or low-sodium vegetable broth

2 plum tomatoes, chopped

8 (6-inch) whole wheat flour tortillas, warmed

1 recipe Creamy Avocado Sauce

Directions:

1. Heat a large nonstick skillet over medium-high heat. Add the oil and tilt the pan to coat the bottom evenly. Add the bell pepper, onion, and jalapeño and cook, stirring often, until softened, 5 minutes. Add the garlic, chili powder, and cumin and cook, stirring constantly, until fragrant, 30 seconds.

2. Add the beans and stock and bring to a boil over high heat. Reduce the heat to low and simmer until the vegetables are tender and most of the liquid has absorbed, about 5 minutes. Add the tomatoes and cook, stirring often, just until heated through, about 3 minutes.

3. Spoon the bean mixture evenly down the center of each tortilla. Roll up and place 2 burritos seam side down on each of 4 plates. Drizzle with the sauce and serve at once.

Nutrition Info:

39 g carb, 364 cal, 11 g fat, 1 g sat fat, 2 mg chol, 25 g fib, 15 g pro, 644 mg sod • Carb Choices: 2 1/2; Exchanges: 2 starch, 1 veg, 1 plant-based protein, 1/2 fat

Corn And Bell Peppers with Thyme

Servings: 6

Ingredients:

2 teaspoons extra virgin olive oil

3 ears corn, kernels cut from the cob

1 small onion, diced

1 small red bell pepper, diced

2 garlic cloves, minced

1/2 cup low-sodium vegetable or chicken broth

1 teaspoon chopped fresh thyme

1/2 teaspoon kosher salt

1/8 teaspoon freshly ground pepper

Directions:

1. Heat a large nonstick skillet over medium-high heat. Add the oil and tilt the pan to coat the bottom evenly. Add the corn, onion, bell pepper, and garlic and cook, stirring frequently, until the vegetables are softened, 5 minutes.

2. Add the broth, thyme, salt, and ground pepper and bring to a boil. Cook, stirring occasionally, until the vegetables are tender and most of the liquid has evaporated, 3 minutes longer. Spoon the vegetables into a serving dish and serve at once.

Nutrition Info:

11 g carb, 64 cal, 2 g fat, 0 g sat fat, 0 mg chol, 2 g fib, 2 g pro, 113 mg sod • Carb Choices: 1/2; Exchanges: 1/2 starch, 1/2 fat

Cornmeal-crusted Fish Fillets

Servings: 4

Ingredients:

1/4 cup yellow cornmeal

4 (5-ounce) thin white-fleshed fish fillets

1/4 teaspoon kosher salt

1/8 teaspoon freshly ground pepper

2 teaspoons extra virgin olive oil

Lemon wedges

Directions:

1. Place the cornmeal on a plate. Sprinkle the fish fillets with the salt and pepper, then dip each one in the cornmeal.

2. Heat a large nonstick skillet over medium heat. Add the oil and tilt the pan to coat the bottom evenly. Add the fish and cook, turning once, until the fish flakes when tested with a fork, about 3 minutes on each side. Divide the fish among 4 plates and serve at once with the lemon wedges.

Nutrition Info:

7 g carb, 166 cal, 4 g fat, 1 g sat fat, 67 mg chol, 1 g fib, 24 g pro, 173 mg sod •
Carb Choices: 1/2; Exchanges: 3 lean protein, 1/2 fat

Asparagus Salad with Orange-ginger Dressing

Servings: 6

Ingredients:

1 1/2 pounds asparagus, tough ends removed

2 tablespoons Orange-Ginger Dressing

2 tablespoons thinly sliced scallions

1/2 teaspoon toasted sesame seeds

Directions:

1. Fill a large saucepan three-fourths full with water; bring to a boil over high heat. Add the asparagus and cook until crisp-tender, 3 to 4 minutes. Drain the asparagus and rinse under cold water until cool. Dry the asparagus with paper towels.

2. Arrange the asparagus on a serving platter. Drizzle with the dressing. Sprinkle with the scallions and sesame seeds and serve at room temperature within 2 hours.

Nutrition Info:

3 g carb, 20 cal, 0 g fat, 0 g sat fat, 0 mg chol, 1 g fib, 1 g pro, 3 mg sod • Carb Choices: 0; Exchanges: 1 veg

Chamomile-ginger Summer Fruit Salad

Servings: 6

Ingredients:

1⁄4 cup sugar

1⁄4 cup water

4 chamomile tea bags

1 cup 1-inch cantaloupe or honeydew melon balls

1 cup 1-inch watermelon balls

1 medium peach, peeled, pitted, and sliced

1⁄2 cup fresh blueberries

2 tablespoons chopped crystallized ginger

Directions:

1. Combine the sugar and water in a small saucepan and bring to a boil over medium heat, stirring until the sugar dissolves. Remove from the heat, add the tea bags, and let stand 30 minutes to cool. Remove and discard the tea bags, squeezing out the liquid.

2. Combine the melon balls, peach slices, and blueberries in a large glass serving bowl. Drizzle with the syrup and toss gently to coat. Sprinkle with the ginger and serve.

Nutrition Info:

16 g carb, 64 cal, 0 g fat, 0 g sat fat, 0 mg chol, 1 g fib, 1 g pro, 5 mg sod • Carb Choices: 1; Exchanges: 1/2 carb, 1/2 fruit

Blistered Cherry Tomatoes with Rosemary

Servings: 4

Ingredients:

3 cups cherry tomatoes

2 teaspoons extra virgin olive oil

2 teaspoons chopped fresh rosemary

1/2 teaspoon grated lemon zest

2 teaspoons lemon juice

1/4 teaspoon kosher salt

Pinch of freshly ground pepper

Directions:

1. Preheat the oven to 425°F.

2. Place the tomatoes on a medium rimmed baking sheet. Drizzle with the oil and stir to coat. Roast until some of the tomatoes burst, 15 to 18 minutes.

3. Transfer the tomatoes and any pan juices to a serving bowl. Add the rosemary, lemon zest, lemon juice, salt, and pepper and stir to coat. Serve hot, warm, or at room temperature.

Nutrition Info:

5 g carb, 42 cal, 3 g fat, 3 g sat fat, 0 mg chol, 1 g fib, 1 g pro, 76 mg sod • Carb Choices: 0; Exchanges: 1 veg, 1/2 fat

Celery–celery Root Soup

Servings: 6

Ingredients:

2 teaspoons extra virgin olive oil

1 medium onion, chopped

2 stalks celery, including some green leaves, chopped

2 garlic cloves, chopped

2 medium celery roots, peeled and chopped (about 6 cups)

1 medium baking potato, peeled and chopped

41/2 to 5 cups Vegetable Stock or low-sodium vegetable broth

3/4 teaspoons kosher salt

2 teaspoons lemon juice

Chopped fresh chives or dill

Directions:

1. Heat a large pot over medium heat. Add the oil and tilt the pan to coat the bottom evenly. Add the onion and celery and cook, stirring often, until softened, 5 minutes. Add the garlic and cook, stirring constantly, until fragrant, 30 seconds. Add the celery roots, potato, 41/2 cups of the stock, and salt and bring to a boil over high heat. Cover, reduce the heat to low, and simmer until the vegetables are very tender, 25 to 30 minutes.

2. Place the celery root mixture in a food processor or blender in batches and process until smooth. Return the soup to the pot and reheat gently over medium heat. Add the remaining 1/2 cup stock a few tablespoons at a time, if needed, to reach the desired consistency. Stir in the lemon juice. Ladle the soup into 6 bowls, sprinkle evenly with the chives, and serve at once. The soup can be refrigerated, covered, for up to 4 days.

Nutrition Info:

22 g carb, 127 cal, 2 g fat, 1 g sat fat, 4 mg chol, 3 g fib, 6 g pro, 388 mg sod • Carb Choices: 11/2; Exchanges: 1/2 starch, 3 veg

Curried Chicken And Winter Vegetable Stew

Servings: 4

Ingredients:

4 teaspoons canola oil, divided

1-pound boneless skinless chicken breast, cut into 1/2-inch cubes

1 medium onion, chopped

2 garlic cloves, minced

1 tablespoon curry powder

31/2 cups Chicken Stock or low-sodium chicken broth

1 (141/2-ounce) can no-added-salt diced tomatoes

1/4 cup no-added-salt tomato paste

2 carrots, peeled, halved lengthwise, and cut into 1-inch slices

1 medium parsnip, peeled, halved lengthwise, and cut into 1-inch slices

1 medium turnip, peeled and chopped

1/4 cup golden raisins

8 ounces fresh spinach, trimmed and chopped

Directions:

1. Heat a large saucepan over medium-high heat. Add 2 teaspoons of the oil and tilt the pan to coat the bottom evenly. Add the chicken and cook, stirring often, until well browned, about 8 minutes. Transfer to a plate.

2. Add the remaining 2 teaspoons oil and tilt the pan to coat the bottom evenly. Add the onion and cook, stirring often, until softened, 5 minutes. Add the garlic and curry powder and cook, stirring constantly, until fragrant, 30 seconds. Add the stock, tomatoes, tomato paste, carrots, parsnip, turnip, raisins, and the chicken and bring to a boil.

3. Cover, reduce the heat to low, and simmer until the vegetables are tender, about 20 minutes. Stir in the spinach and cook just until wilted, 2 minutes. Ladle the stew evenly into 4 bowls and serve at once. The stew can be refrigerated, covered, for up to 4 days.

Nutrition Info:

32 g carb, 325 cal, 8 g fat, 2 g sat fat, 67 mg chol, 7 g fib, 31 g pro, 315 mg sod •
Carb Choices: 2; Exchanges: 1/2 starch, 1/2 carb, 3 veg, 3 lean protein, 1 fat

Black Bean And Roasted Red Pepper Quesadillas

Servings: 2

Ingredients:

1/2 cup canned no-salt-added black beans, rinsed and drained

1/4 cup red Roasted Bell Peppers or roasted red peppers from a jar, chopped

1 ounce shredded reduced-fat Monterey Jack cheese (about 1/4 cup)

2 tablespoons thinly sliced scallion

2 tablespoons chopped fresh cilantro

4 (6-inch) whole wheat flour tortillas

1 teaspoon canola oil

1/2 cup Fresh Tomato Salsa or purchased salsa

Directions:

1. Combine the beans, roasted peppers, Monterey Jack, scallion, and cilantro in a medium bowl and stir to mix well.

2. Brush one side of each of the tortillas with the oil. Place two of the tortillas oiled side down on a work surface. Top the tortillas evenly with the bean mixture. Cover with the remaining two tortillas, oiled side up.

3. Heat a large nonstick skillet over medium-high heat. Add one of the quesadillas and cook until the tortillas are lightly browned and the cheese melts, about 2 minutes on each side. Repeat with the remaining quesadilla. Cut the quesadillas into wedges and serve each one with 1/4 cup of the salsa.

Nutrition Info:

35 g carb, 317 cal, 12 g fat, 5 g sat fat, 13 mg chol, 20 g fib, 14 g pro, 701 mg sod •
Carb Choices: 2; Exchanges: 2 starch, 1 veg, 2 fat

Yogurt Tartar Sauce

Servings: 1/2 Cup

Ingredients:

1/4 cup mayonnaise

1/4 cup plain low-fat yogurt

1 tablespoon finely minced scallion, white part only

1 tablespoon minced fresh Italian parsley

2 teaspoons sweet pickle relish

2 teaspoons lemon juice

1/2 teaspoon Dijon mustard

1/8 teaspoon kosher salt

Directions:

1. Stir together all the ingredients in a small bowl. The sauce can be refrigerated, covered, for up to 3 days.

Nutrition Info:

1 g carb, 58 cal, 6 g fat, 1 g sat fat, 3 mg chol, 0 g fib, 0 g pro, 79 mg sod • Carb Choices: 0; Exchanges: 1 fat

Linguini And Tomatoes with Creamy Ricotta Sauce

Servings: 4

Ingredients:

6 ounces whole wheat linguini or other long, thin pasta

2/3 cup part-skim ricotta

1 ounce (about 1/4 cup) plus 2 tablespoons freshly grated Parmesan, divided

1/4 cup chopped fresh basil

1 garlic clove, crushed through a press

1/4 teaspoon kosher salt

1/8 teaspoon freshly ground pepper

2 large tomatoes, chopped

Directions:

1. Cook the pasta according to the package directions. Drain and keep warm, reserving 1/3 cup of the cooking water.

2. Meanwhile, stir together the ricotta, 1/4 cup of the Parmesan, the basil, garlic, salt, and pepper in a large bowl. Add the hot pasta and toss to coat. Add the reserved pasta cooking water 1 tablespoon at a time, as needed, to make a smooth sauce. Add the tomatoes and toss gently to combine.

3. To serve, divide the pasta mixture evenly among 4 plates. Sprinkle evenly with the remaining 2 tablespoons Parmesan and serve at once.

Nutrition Info:

37 g carb, 252 cal, 6 g fat, 3 g sat fat, 19 mg chol, 6 g fib, 15 g pro, 245 mg sod •
Carb Choices: 2; Exchanges: 1 1/2 starch, 1 veg, 1 medium-fat protein

Butternut Squash Soup with Red Curry And Coconut

Servings: 6

Ingredients:

2 teaspoons extra virgin olive oil

1 medium onion, chopped

2 garlic cloves, minced

1 medium butternut squash, peeled, seeded, and chopped (about 5 cups)

2 1/2 to 3 cups Vegetable Stock or low-sodium vegetable broth

1/2 teaspoon kosher salt

1 teaspoon red curry paste

1/3 cup reduced-fat coconut milk

2 teaspoons lime juice

Directions:

1. Heat a large saucepan over medium heat. Add the oil and tilt the pan to coat the bottom evenly. Add the onion and cook, stirring often, until softened, 5 minutes. Add the garlic and cook, stirring constantly, until fragrant, 30 seconds. Add the squash, 2 1/2 cups of the stock, and salt and bring to a boil over high heat. Cover, reduce the heat to low, and simmer until the squash is very tender, 15 to 20 minutes.

2. Place the squash mixture in a food processor or blender in batches, adding the curry paste to one of the batches, and process until smooth. Return the soup to the pot, stir in the coconut milk, and reheat gently over medium heat. Stir in the lime juice. Ladle the soup into 6 bowls and serve at once. The soup can be refrigerated, covered, for up to 4 days or frozen for up to 3 months.

Nutrition Info:

19 g carb, 110 cal, 4 g fat, 3 g sat fat, 0 mg chol, 3 g fib, 2 g pro, 216 mg sod • Carb Choices: 1; Exchanges: 1 starch, 1 veg

Rosemary White Bean Dip with Artichokes

Servings: 2 Cups

Ingredients:

1 (14-ounce) can artichoke hearts

1 (15-ounce) can no-salt-added cannellini beans, rinsed and drained

1 small garlic clove, chopped

2 tablespoons extra virgin olive oil

2 tablespoons lemon juice

2 teaspoons minced fresh rosemary

1/8 teaspoon freshly ground pepper

Directions:

1. Drain the artichoke hearts and cut into halves. Place the artichokes on several thicknesses of paper towels and gently blot dry.

2. Combine the artichoke hearts and the remaining ingredients in a food processor and process until smooth.

3. Transfer to a serving bowl and serve at once, or refrigerate, covered, for up to 3 days.

Nutrition Info:

13 g carb, 104 cal, 4 g fat, 1 g sat fat, 0 mg chol, 4 g fib, 4 g pro, 319 mg sod • Carb Choices: 1; Exchanges: 1/2 starch, 1 veg, 1 fat

Chicken Pot-au-feu

Servings: 6

Ingredients:

1 whole chicken (about 3 1/4 pounds), skinned

6 cups Chicken Stock or low-sodium chicken broth

1 small sprig fresh thyme or 1/4 teaspoon dried thyme

1 bay leaf

1/4 teaspoon kosher salt

1/4 teaspoon freshly ground pepper

1 medium leek, halved lengthwise and thinly sliced

8 ounces baby potatoes, well scrubbed

8 ounces baby carrots

2 parsnips, peeled and cut into 1-inch slices

2 small zucchinis, halved lengthwise and sliced

1/4 cup chopped fresh Italian parsley

Directions:

1. Place the chicken in a large pot. Add the stock, thyme, bay leaf, salt, and pepper. Bring to a boil over high heat, cover, reduce the heat to low, and simmer 20 minutes.

2. Meanwhile, submerge the sliced leek in a bowl of water, lift it out, and drain in a colander. Repeat, using fresh water, until no grit remains in the bowl. Drain the leek well.

3. Add the leek, potatoes, carrots, and parsnips to the pot. Return to a simmer and cook until the vegetables are tender and the juices of the chicken run clear, 25 minutes longer. Add the zucchini and simmer until crisp-tender, 2 to 3 minutes. Remove and discard the thyme sprig and bay leaf.

4. Transfer the chicken to a cutting board and carve. Stir the parsley into the stock mixture. Divide the chicken, vegetables, and broth evenly among 6 large shallow bowls.

Nutrition Info:

23 g carb, 257 cal, 4 g fat, 1 g sat fat, 86 mg chol, 5 g fib, 32 g pro, 319 mg sod •
Carb Choices: 1 1/2; Exchanges: 1 starch, 1 veg, 4 lean protein

Alphabetical Index

F

G

L

O

R

S

T

W

CPSIA information can be obtained
at www.ICGtesting.com
Printed in the USA
LVHW022032070621
689597LV00016B/2091

9 781803 100227